101 AWESOME THINGS YOU MUST DO IN

CUBA

James Hall

101 AWESOME THINGS YOU MUST DO IN CUBA

For information visit:
http://www.JamesHallTravel.com

ISBN-10: 1546598383
ISBN-13 : 978-1546598381

First Edition: May 2017
10 9 8 7 6 5 4 3 2 1

CONTENTS

Foreword

So, you want to go to Cuba, do you? Absolutely you do! Who doesn't?

Cuba is an elusive land of coconut and old-fashioned cars. Not to mention that it has the appeal of the forbidden fruit. In the 1960s, due to a trade embargo that made travel nearly impossible, travel to Cuba was banned for American citizens. So, from that point on, Cuba remained an elusive land of mystery rather than a travel destination.

However—Cuba dreamers rejoice! Recently, due to new regulations from the federal government, there are now regular flights between Cuba and the United States, and you can plan yourself a trip! This doesn't mean that it's a totally open border, there are certainly still more than a handful of things you need to consider and manage appropriately before you travel.

However, this does mean that all that dreaming you've been doing about Cuba can finally come to fruition! There is so much to do in this beautiful country and very few people have had the chance to experience it.

Chase your dream onto this Caribbean Island—drink rum, eat incredible food, and listen to amazing music. In this book, I have this awesome list of suggestions of Cuba staple destinations, as well as some odd excursions that might not be on your radar – yet!

So sit back, relax with some coconut water and let's talk about Cuba!

Chapter 1: History Lesson

The U.S. has a long and complicated history with Cuba and it will behoove you to have an idea of that history before you get there. While you're actually there, you may find that it doesn't come into play all that much.

People aren't really walking around giving history quizzes or anything, but the details of this relationship between the United States and Cuba are very important to be aware of as you are preparing to go. Before you go you'll want to know these things.

1) Know where you are going to

You are going to the Republic of Cuba, a Caribbean island nation less than 300 miles from the coast of Florida. The tropical climate is only part of the appeal—the white sandy beaches, sugar cane and tobacco fields are all iconic elements of the country. Though locationally Caribbean, Cuba is culturally considered Latin American, so you will see evidence of influence and customs from many surrounding countries.

Since 1965, Cuba has been governed by the Communist Party of Cuba, and you will see in any reading you do that the tumultuous political climate of the last one hundred years has had a huge effect on the culture, community and customs of the Cuban people and lifestyle. It has certainly played a big role in the relationship between the country and the United States, as well as other nations. You will encounter and perhaps even plan visits to many monuments and memorials for their long political hardships.

2) Know how you will communicate

The official language of Cuba is Spanish, so it would be in your absolute best interest to learn the basics of the language to help you navigate around the country. You don't have to become fluent, but I suggest learning enough so that you can ask for directions and look for the landmarks you are trying to find.

Also, keep in mind that are different versions of Spanish that are spoken throughout the world and the specific dialect used in Cuba may be unfamiliar, even to those of you who speak another Spanish dialect. Look into all of this before your trip—it will help immensely and make your trip all the more enjoyable.

3) What's the fuss?

Why is it so hard to get to Cuba? Well, the United States has a long history with Cuba that hasn't always made it easy for travel between the two countries. Conflicts—such as the Cuban Missile Crisis in 1962 and the Trade Embargo in 1960—led to restrictions on travel and trade. As a result, travel was restricted between the United States and Cuba. Actually, the physical act of travel itself wasn't restricted, but monetary transaction with Cuba was, which made a trip there nearly impossible. Realistically, you wouldn't even be able to get there! Very recently, restrictions have begun to be lifted and limited imports and travel is being accepted once again.

What does all of this mean for you? It means that travel to Cuba doesn't have to be only a dream. It has begun to shift into the realm of reality for more and more Americans. However, there are still come serious considerations you must keep in mind as you are planning your trip.

Chapter 2: Getting Ready

Now that you know a little more know about the country you are planning to visit, you have to actually get it all together and plan your trip!

Because of the sensitive relationship between the US and Cuba, you'll want to take some extra care in the planning—you don't want to miss something important, as it might cost you your entire trip!

Read this portion of my guide very carefully, but definitely also do some research on your own. Double check the current standing of the travel laws and visa restrictions. These things can change at any time and you absolutely must be prepared, for your own best interest. Read well, do more research, and you should be good to go!

4) Know if you can go.

Check the governmental travel restrictions and guidelines before you go. As of January 27, 2017, the United States Department of Passports and International travel still deemed travel to Cuba to be prohibited. To travel to Cuba, one must obtain a license from the Department of Treasury or fall into one of the following 12 categories, listed on the government website. (Be sure to check it before you go as things can change frequency https://travel.state.gov/content/passports/en/cou ntry/cuba.html.)

1. Family visits

2. Official business of the U.S. government, foreign governments, and certain intergovernmental organizations

3. Journalistic activity

4. Professional research and professional meetings

5. Educational activities

6. Religious activities

7. Public performances, clinics, workshops, athletic and other competitions, and exhibitions

8. Support for the Cuban people

9. Humanitarian projects

10. Activities of private foundations or research or educational institutes

11. Exportation, importation, or transmission of information or informational materials

12. Certain authorized export transactions.

Let's assume that if you are planning a trip to Cuba you are going for one of the above reasons, you know the restrictions, and you are prepared for the trip ahead. Congratulations! Now you just have to prepare.

5) Have a Visa plan.

You must have a Visa to travel into Cuba and to return home. Some airlines allow you to purchase your visa along with your airfare or at the airport. The prices on these vary depending on what airline you fly or if you buy it separately. Don't wait to get this very important step taken care of. You don't want to end up stranded because you forgot to plan.

6) Money, money, money.

Get your money in order. There are two

different currencies in Cuba. The Cuban Convertible Peso and the Cuban Peso. When you exchange currency in the country, you will be given the Cuban Convertible Peso as it is considered the tourist currency.

Before you go, look into the currency exchange rates so you have an idea of how much your local money will be worth in Cuba. It's always better to plan and budget before you get there so there are no surprises when you arrive.

This is also a very important issue to double check before you enter the country. **For many years, even with modest travel allowances into Cuba, United States credit cards would not work there. You had to bring your money in cash and exchange it there.** There has been some lightening of this law and currently credit cards are not entirely shut down in Cuba. However, the official government website does still advise travelers to be prepared to use only cash, so you need to have a plan for this and confirm the current standings of cash allowances and credit card capabilities before you enter the country.

It would be prudent to bring cash with you even if you believe you will be able to use your credit card, just as a precaution. Your trip isn't going to be any fun if you don't have the resources you need to eat, drink or travel.

7) Know the weather.

Due to its location, Cuba generally experiences temperate, tropical climates all year-round. That being said, it is always in your best interest to look into the weather conditions before you travel to a new location, that way you can pack appropriately. Make sure to bring sunscreen and some bright, festive clothes so you can blend it, but not burn.

8) Plan your stay.

Because Havana is the primary destination of trips to Cuba, hotels can get very pricey in the city.

Look around before you buy to try and get the best deal. If you are open to it, you can also explore the possibilities of homestays—staying in the home of a local at a much lesser cost. As always, make sure it is a reputable place and that someone knows where you are and how to contact you while you are gone. Saving money is great, but safety comes first!

Chapter 3: Classic Cuba

It's hard to explain, but Cuba just has a 'vibe.' There is something about the music, the cars, the colors, and the weather, that is so... well... cool. No matter how long you are staying, or for what purpose you are there, there are a handful of classic Cuban activities you will absolutely need to participate in before you head home. I listed some of these awesome activities below. But remember, no list is ever complete—the best part of visiting any country is finding your own favorite activity or location that you could never have anticipated or planned for!

9) Check out the cars.

Walking or driving around Cuba looks like a scene right out of the history books. The entire country looks as if it got left behind in time, if for no other reason than the old-style American cars. While it makes Cuba look very classy, this is actually rooted in some very real explanations.

Quite frankly, purchasing international automobiles or parts is forbidden, so time moves on, but the cars stay the same. It adds a lot of ambience and style, so it's not necessarily a bad thing.

10) Listen to live music.

All over Cuba, the streets, the bars and the restaurants are bursting with music, typically salsa and jazz. Full of life, story and emotion, there is so much to take in and appreciate about the music scene in Cuba. If you don't set some time aside to stop and listen, you'll definitely regret it in the end.

Music holds in its very essence, the power to take you to a place. The music in Cuba seems to keep you there. With just a few notes played in the right way, you are totally immersed in the culture and the community. You may even find a new favorite and you may want to stay forever!

11) Learn how to salsa.

Once you have been inspired by the music and the attitude, it's time for you to step up and learn some new steps. If you're really doing Cuba right, you are salsa dancing through the night (mojito in hand, I would imagine). There are places where you can book yourself salsa dancing lessons or if you're feeling more adventurous you could just jump right in with the locals and learn from them. The style in which you learn is up to you—but it really should be high on your priority list.

12) Go to a baseball game.

Baseball is the national sport and the beloved pastime of Cuba—there is so much love for this sport in this country. Going to see a game is a trip in and of itself, and you will remember the energy, the excitement and the momentum forever!

But don't go looking for the next up and coming Major League Baseball player, because you won't find one. It is illegal for the United States to recruit baseball players from Cuba. So, you will just have to enjoy them for their talent right where they are. But the one thing I can say for sure is that you don't want to miss the chance to see a game.

13) Go to the beach.

I mean really, how could you not? The beaches in Cuba are divine and they are at least half of the appeal of the country as it is. Whether you like to spend the whole day basking in the sun, or just prefer a leisurely walk in the sand watching the waves, it doesn't matter.

You will fall in love with the beautiful sight of that so blue ocean and very white sand. It is paradise right before your eyes. The only problem with Cuban beaches is that once you are there you may never want to leave.

14) Eat raw sugar cane.

It's the best in the world! Grab yourself a stick of sugar cane and chew on it to release the raw sugar. This is the flavor that runs our world! That is, if you have a sweet tooth like I do! You can even get fresh sugar cane juiced and drink the perfectly sweet juice that comes out. Better than sugar water, you'll keep going back for more and more.

15) See a tobacco field.

There is a reason that Cuban cigars are

coveted—they are the best of the best, and when it comes to the best of the best with cigars—you have to start with tobacco. Down in the Vinales Valley you can see the fields and get a sense of what the tobacco looks like, right from the source.

16) Take a motorcycle tour.

With Che no less! No, not the iconic revolutionary leader, but his youngest son. Ernesto Guevara will take you across Cuba on Harley Davidsons—surely an incredible and one of a kind tour. If you are a biker, this is a tour you definitely don't want to miss. On the flipside, as cool as it sounds, it is not recommended for anyone who isn't already comfortable writing a motorcycle. Seems like a given, but worth a mention, just in case!

17) Try snorkeling.

Just by looking at the pristine oceans that

surround the island of Cuba, you know there must be some pretty incredible life happening under the water. And sure enough there is, and you can see it. Off the shores of Cuba are great places to snorkel and see the incredible marine life active and alive all around you. Get up close and personal with the beauty of the island and experience a breathtaking view of it all.

18) Ride in a taxi.

If you are into the cars of Cuba, take the opportunity to ride in one! The taxis of the city are no exception to the cool car rule. You can ride around in style and get to your desired destination. It's a win-win all the way.

19) Swim in a cenote.

When the weather is warm you can cool down in a cenote— a sinkhole caused by collapsed limestone that exposes underground water. It's a beautiful natural phenomenon and Cuba is one of the few places in the world where you can experience it! What an awesome way to cool off and experience one of the great wonders of this land. I can't recommend this enough.

20) Watch the crab crossing.

If you are visiting the Bay of Pigs you may come across a giant group of crabs crossing the road. There are often so many that they create a massive road block. If you're not in a hurry this can be an awesome experience and absolute must-do photo opportunity!

21) Chase a waterfall. Stand in awe of the beauty of the Vegas Grande waterfall around Toped de Collantes. You could even dip a toe in and go for a swim! The incredible beauty of this waterfall is something you certainly don't want to miss. It is majestic and memorable.

22) Ride a bull.

If you go on a tour of the Vinales tobacco fields you will have the opportunity to choose your tour to be either by bull, carriage or horseback. You have a premium decision to make. And let's be honest, you should probably choose the bull.

23) Smoke a Cuban cigar.

Now, I totally understand that this isn't going to be everyone's cup of tea, but it seems nearly impossible to talk about Cuba and not address one of their most famous products. Cuban cigars are coveted for their superior tobacco and flavor, and because of the trade laws they are not easy to get outside of the country.

This trip may well be one of your few chances to ever smoke a true Cuban cigar. Cigar aficionados all over the world hold these products in the highest regard, so I suggest you seize the opportunity if you have the interest in partaking. And if you do—enjoy!

Chapter 4: Havana

So, you have finally made it to Cuba. It hasn't been easy for you to get here so you want to be sure and see all the amazing places that you've always dreamed of!

This all starts in Havana, how could it not? Havana is the Capital of Cuba and a bustling, lively city of beautiful colors, incredible music and unforgettable culture. Your wildest dreams come true in Havana. Let's get started on a list of what you simply cannot miss while you are there!

24) Explore Old Havana.

The city center and the hub of Havana—Old Havana—is a no-brainer. Here you will explore the ins and outs of the city. Old Havana is bursting with stories, pastel painted houses, authentic meals to be enjoyed and classic drinks to be consumed. There is live music nearly everywhere and this is the heart and soul of the city. Take your time wandering around and meandering through. You'll likely discover a few favorite places to return to over and over.

25) Walk along Malecon.

The Malecon is a wide esplanade that stretches the Havana coast from Havana Harbor to Old Havana. It's a beautiful walk along the seawall and a fantastic place to stretch your legs and get some sightseeing in all at the same time. Although this is an incredible place to visit at any time of the day, it is a must-see at sunset, when the lights of the city and the reflections in the water are their most beautiful. It is picture perfect.

26) See Morro Castle.

This fortress guarding the entrance to the Havana Bay was named after the three biblical Magi and is definitely worthy of a visit during your travels. Anything with the word castle in the title is typically intriguing and there are undoubtedly a whole host of stories and legends to learn of.

27) Visit the Capital.

The National Capitol Building in Havana, also known as El Capitolio, was the primary seat of government in Cuba until after the Cuban Revolution in 1959, and today is the home of the Cuban Academy of Sciences. Many important moments in Cuban history occurred right in this place. Take a walk around and see if you too feel inspired for change.

28) See Giant Jesus.

If you take the time to visit the Christ of Havana, you'll be awed by the giant statue of Jesus that stands on a hillside overlooking the bay. This immense statue is the work of Jilma Madera, a Cuban sculptor who won a commission for his work on this project in 1953. The tall sculpture stands over everyone who comes to see and has a majestic presence that is absolutely worthy of a visit.

29) See an optical illusion.

On the top floor of the Edificio Gomaz Villa in the Plaza Vieji is the famous "Camera Obsura" of Havana. Invented by Leonardo da Vinci, this is an optical device that provides to its viewer a live 360 degree view of the entire city. It is an incredible way to see Havana, one you will certainly remember for the rest of your life!

30) Relax on a rooftop.

If you swing by the Hotel Ambos Mundos, you can grab a drink on their notorious rooftop bar the famed writer Ernest Hemingway was said to have frequented during his time in Havana. The hotel was built in 1924 and remains a fabulous testament to the design and architecture of its time. While you're here you should try one of the many classic cocktails that originated in Cuba. There is certainly no shortage of options to choose from. Enjoy the history, the rum and the view.

31) Go to church.

The Havana Cathedral is one of eleven Roman Catholic Cathedrals that exist on the island of Cuba. Located in the center of Old Havana, this cathedral was described by novelist Alejo Carpentier as "music set in stone," a testament to the beauty of this baroque style cathedral. Experience the living music that abounds in this place. Enjoy the architecture and the elaborate design.

32) See some art.

At the Museum of Decorative Arts there is a wide variety of art that you can enjoy offering a unique insight to wealth, culture and history of the city of Havana. The museum itself was the home of former resident Countess Maria Luisa Gomes Mena viuda de Cagiga. With a name so long, you know there are stories of her just waiting for you to discover them!

33) See the fish.

Sure, there a lot of them surrounding the island, but there are a good amount on the island itself, at the National Aquarium of Cuba located in Havana. The museum was established in 1960 with the intent to focus on research and environmental education—a noble cause! Displayed at the museum are various tropical species and coral. It is a fabulous experience and an opportunity to see what exists in the ocean all around the island of Cuba. This is a fun excursion, especially if you are not the snorkeling type but still want to experience the amazing life forms that surround beautiful Cuba.

34) Go to the zoo.

The Jardin Zoo has a long history and is a great activity if you are traveling with young children. If you are here with your family, you may be looking for activities that involve less lively rum and more family fun. In that case, this is the perfect destination for you, because in addition to the great variety of animals that are displayed at the zoo, there is also a small train for children to ride. They, and you, are sure to enjoy your time here—who doesn't love the zoo!

35) Buy some books.

If the first thing you do when you get to Cuba is go on a search for Hemingway's old hang-out, you're probably a fan of books so you'll also be a fan of this plaza! The Plaza de Armas is the oldest plaza in the city and it is surrounded by restaurants and book stands. It's pretty much a readers dream come true: Cuba, food and books. What more could a person ask for?

36) Learn about rum.

If you read the previous suggestion and just weren't really feeling it, and were left feeling like— yeah, I could ask for more than a bunch of book stands... maybe this is the destination for you. The Museo del Ron Havana Club is a museum dedicated to the history of making rum in Cuba and even includes a tasting room and a liquor shop. It's both educational and delicious. If you're interested in the rum culture of Cuba, you are sure to enjoy this stop on your trip!

37) Watch "El Canonazo de las nueve."

This beautiful tradition is one you'll want to see while you are in Havana. At 9 pm sharp, soldiers gather in the fortress of La Cabana, wearing traditional 18th century costumes and shooting canons in a traditional warning to close the city gates. If you need another reason to go and watch—besides the beautiful history—your admission ticket includes a drink! This is an age old tradition and it is truly an incredible opportunity to be a part of it.

38) See the most eclectic square.

The Plaza Vieja was laid out in 1559. This old and beautiful square is the most architecturally eclectic square in all of Havana. It was originally used for military exercises and in later years was used as an open-air market. Today, it's a hub of culture and movement. It even has its own microbrewery! With an evolution like that you know that the plaza has stood the test of time and likely will for years to come. The only thing to wonder is what will it become next? Go see it now so you can be a part of its long history.

39) Go to the Tropicana Club.

Easily, the most well known club and cabaret in Havana, the Tropicana opened in 1939 at Villa Mina, an old estate with lush, tropical gardens. It became such a hit that spin-offs can be found in big cities such as New York and Atlantic City. But nothing is as good as the original. The food, the music, the ambience—this is a place you absolutely can't miss while you are in Havana.

Chapter 5: Food Staples

There is a lot to see and enjoy while you are in Cuba, but don't discount how much there is to eat! And certainly don't discount how delicious it all is. There are new spins on food you already know and love, as well entirely new entrees that will have you asking for more, more, more!

You'll want to plan a good portion of your trip around the food you'll be eating! Get ready—there is a lot of good stuff coming your way! Eat, drink and be merry, you're in Cuba!

40) Tamales.

Now, I grew up eating tamales every Christmas so I didn't think this could be anything new or exciting. But Cuban tamales are distinctly different than Mexican tamales, and they are nothing to take for granted! Rather than masa with a filling, Cuban tamales have all of their ingredients mixed together and are a tasty treat for any day!

41) Medianoche.

The name of this delicious sandwich literally

means 'midnight' and that's because it is often served in nightclubs. The sweet bread is filled with ham, pork, cheese and pickles, and it surely makes a delicious midnight snack. You might find that you are going out to clubs at night, not for the music and drinks but for the delicious food that comes out when the sun goes down!

42) Congri.

Very simple and simply perfect, this is a staple eaten with any number of meals. It's a flavorful blend of white rice, black beans and the perfect harmony of different spices. This can be a side or a meal all unto itself and you'll certainly be looking for more as soon as you finish.

43) Vaca Frita.

Literally meaning 'fried cow,' this Cuban specialty consists of seasoned, seared beef, cooked to a near crispy perfection. I wasn't sure at first if this was appealing or not, but trust me, it is and you definitely want to try it.

44) Paella.

Now, I know what you're thinking—Paella is a very classic traditional Spanish dish. But Cuba put their own spin on it and really made it their own. Besides the fabulous mix of spices and flavors, it includes ham, chicken, mussels, chorizo, shrimp, scallops and lobster. What more could you possibly want?

45) Shrimp in coconut sauce.

My perfect meal—this absolutely divine dish combined the delicate and distinct flavors of coconut with fresh shrimp. There is something so wonderful about eating a dish in which both of the main ingredients come fresh from the country that they are served in.

46) Huevo habaneros.

This delicious egg dish can be enjoyed any time of the day—consisting of eggs served over sofrita, which is a fried mixture of tomatoes, garlic, peppers and onions. A simple egg dish has never has so much flavor and personality! You'll be looking for this one over and over.

47) Lechon asado.

A classic—this meal will have your mouth watering for more. To make this dish, the pig is cooked whole on a spit until the skin is crispy and delicious. Often this pork dish is served with the Cuban 'mojo' sauce. You'll never find this dish replicated quite the same way anywhere else in the world.

48) Corn on the cob.

Sound simple? It is, but it is so worth it. The

grilled corn is rolled in cojita cheese and sprinkled with chili powder and lime juice, making it the perfect blend of sweet, spicy and acidic. You'll never want to go back to eating plain corn.

49) Chicarrones.

There's not much to say about this dish except that it is fried pork rinds. It salty, crispy and unexpectedly addicting. Not exactly going onto your health food list, but there is no doubt that once you try these you'll want more and more.

50) Yuca fingers.

More fried deliciousness—in this dish, large chunks of yuca are fried in oil for a perfect crunch and snack. Fried isn't always better, but sometimes, it definitely is.

51) Plantains.

These are a staple for just about any meal, so during your time in Cuba you're sure to eat them more than one way! They are served with eggs and hash, they are served fried, they are served as 'maduros' which means cooked in oil until they are caramelized. Whatever way they are served, you are sure to enjoy them!

Chapter 6: Drink it up!

Now that you know what you'll be eating while you're there—let's get to the really important issues. What are you going to drink while you are there? There is no shortage of options! Cuba is known for their rum, so you can bet that at least a few of your beverage options will include it!

If you find a favorite, you could stick with it for the rest of your trip, or you could try a little bit of everything while you are there and really try the whole range.

52) Coconut water.

No rum in this one—pure, fresh coconut, straight out of the shell. This refreshing drink is a Cuban staple and one that is not to be missed. Slightly sweet and completely delicious, you'll be going back to this over and over.

53) Daiquiri.

Rum, ice, lemon, sugar and a variety of different flavor options—this is a delicious favorite.

54) Mojito.

This is my favorite of all the drinks in Cuba. It is the perfect blend of rum, sparkling water, sugar, lemon or lime juice, ice and mint. The most refreshing drink on a summer day and noted as the favorite drink of Ernest Hemingway. A mojito is a must have.

55) Cuba libre.

Rum and coke with a squeeze of lemon. A fabulous and refreshing twist on a favorite mix of flavors.

56) Pina colada.

This drink didn't originate in Cuba, but it has certainly been perfected there! Pineapple juice and coconut milk—what more could you ask for in this beautiful Cuban climate?!

57) Cubanito.

This zesty cocktail includes both Worcestershire and hot sauce, so it's practically part of your meal and will certainly leave a bold impression on you.

58) President.

Not surprisingly, there is additional rum in this one, mixed with black vermouth, grenadine and ice, then served with cherries and an orange peel. A classic Cuban cocktail.

59) Saoco.

This is just plain fun to drink! A simple combination of coconut milk and either sugar cane, brandy, or rum, once this drink is mixed for you it is actually served in the coconut. It tastes better just for that one simple fact!

60) Havana loco.

The name says it all! The crazy Havana! Clearly this mixture has to include rum! Mixed with a selection of rich tropical fruit and you have a tropical flavor deluxe drink that you'll be happy to be sipping on for the duration of your trip.

Chapter 7: Off the Beaten Path

When I think about Cuba, it's those classic cars, beautiful colors and fresh cold coconut water—all the things we've already discussed. But there are a whole slew of other possibilities when you are planning your trip that I seriously think you should consider. A lot of these are a little dark, but all are absolutely fascinating. I think you'll find that you are surprised by how many of these odd places you'll want to see in person!

61) Visit a secret underground dance club.

La Cueva, or 'The Cave' is a dance club located 100 feet underground right outside the city of

Trinidad. This might be the place that you would least expect a bustling dance club, as the city above ground feels like the land of long ago—horses on cobblestone streets and what not.

Not exactly the place that comes to mind when you think about booming Top 40's music. People come from all over to partake in the nightlife in this most unusual of places.

The thing is—the music isn't even the most unusual thing about this cave! Rumor has it that this cave is the setting of a very unsettling past. Serial killer Carlos Ayala used to live in this cave, and this may not be my first choice of warm and fuzzy places, but it certainly seems to draw a crowd, so the mystery and history must be interesting to some. Or, at the very least, the drinks and the music must be really good.

62) See a rock concert at an old estate.

La Tropical Brewery used to be an eloquent

estate, hosting black tie events and socialite gatherings. But time and not enough use to fund maintenance has led to this estate falling into disrepair. Although many have tried to bring the fabulous grounds back to what they once were, no one has had success. The land now belongs to the Havana Metropolitan Parks Organization and frequent rock concerts are hosted there. Not quite as demure, but still quite lively!

63) Go nuclear.

Take the opportunity to visit the abandoned site of a nuclear power plant. Started in 1976, when Cuba and the Soviet Union agreed to co-manage the plant, the site has been abandoned since the fall of the Soviet Union in 1992. It is an eerie site of half baked plans and no real resolution, but it is testament to changing times.

64) Go directly to jail.

Just visiting of course. Not quite the Monopoly jail scene—Presidio Modelo is the model prison. Built in 1928 by Gerardo Machado, the prison closed in 1966 and is now a museum.

The idea of the circular prisons cells is that with the shadowed watchtower, the prisoners would never know if they were being watched and would live in constant unease. It's an uncomfortable reality and an uncomfortable idea. Today you can go look at the grounds of the model prison.

65) Visit a cemetery. Named after Christopher Columbus, "Cemetario de Cristobal Colon" is a pristine cemetery in the heart of Havana. In the center of it all is a cathedral that is fashioned after the beautiful Duomo in the center of Florence, Italy. The beautiful domed cathedral is a lovely center point of this elaborate resting place. The final resting places are organized by rank and order of social class, so you can tell a lot about a person by where he or she spends the rest of their

eternity. The first person to ever rest in the cemetery was its own designer, Loira, who died before its completion.

66) Fusterlandia.

What's that you ask? This eccentric and fun to pronounce neighborhood is the culmination of art by Fuster that expands throughout a Cuban neighborhood. Once riddled with poverty, it is now riddled with colorful, elaborate art. A walk around Fusterlandia is sure to bring you joy.

67) Have a moment with Hemingway.

Hemingway. The great elusive man who changed American literature for the century. There has never been another writer quite like Hemingway and it is likely there never will be. You can visit the house—Finca Vigia—where he wrote Old Man and the Sea and For Whom the Bell Tolls. Maybe standing in the very place where he wrote these masterpieces, you'll find a little inspiration of your own!

68) Have a Barcardi.

Wait— didn't we already address the fact that you should drink rum while you are in Cuba? Good. Let's just reiterate. You are in Cuba—drink rum! While you're at it you should go check out the iconic Barcardi Building, generally renowned as a masterpiece of art deco. Although Barcardi no longer uses this building as their headquarters, it is still a worthwhile spot to see the incredible architecture and design that came out of that era.

69) Sit with John Lennon.

Although the music of John Lennon and the rest of the Beatles was officially banned in the 60s and 70s, there is now bronze statue of the musician in Cuba—set by Castro to honor a fellow dreamer. Today, you can sit by Lennon on a bench in a park dedicated to his memory.

70) Check out Lenin.

The name might sound the same, but there is a different Lenin statue you could also see while you are in Cuba. After the death of the revolutionary communist Vladimir Lenin, an olive tree was planted in his honor on a hillside in Havana. This was the first monument to Lenin outside of the USSR. But it wasn't appreciated by all. In 1930 the olive tree was cut down by a group protesting the dictatorship of Cuba. The protestors have had a harder time removing the bronze statue that was put up on the hillside in 1968. It remains there today as a tribute and monument.

71) Get familiar with the railway.

The railway in Cuba has a long history, as it is the primary means to transport goods throughout the country. Cuba was the first Latin American country to have a railway and it was used for the expansive exportation of sugar. Today the original railway models are up for display at the Steam Engine Museum in Havana. Locomotive fans will enjoy this walk through railway history!

72) Get revolutionary.

It goes without saying that much of what you will see and hear in Cuba is related to their tumultuous history. If you are in Cuba, you may well be familiar and fascinated by this history already. If that is the case, you'll almost certainly want to visit La Plaza de la Revolution. One of the largest city squares in the world—Revolution Square is host to a lot of history and one of the world's most iconic images—of Che on the wall. You've seen this image replicated all over the world in innumerous different platforms, but the chance to see the original work is one that you really should not pass up!

73) Learn more about Che.

After you've seen his face, larger than life in the wall at Revolution Hall, you might want to learn more about the revolutionary leader—Che. If that is the case, be sure to visit his final resting spot at the Che Guevara Mausoleum. This has become a revered resting place of honor and people from all over the world go to pay their respects to the leader.

74) Stay, or at least visit this elaborate hotel!

The National Hotel of Cuba is one of the finest hotels in the entire world and has a history as elaborate as the design! Since it was built, the hotel has attracted elite guests and that continues to this day. The building has remained standing and intact through a number of wars and various time of crisis—like invasions of various foreign armies, pirate attacks—you name it! This hotel is where Castro held his headquarters during the Cuban Missile Crisis in 1962. You can still see traces of the trenches dug around the property during that time period, although today it is back to being an elite hotel and looks a lot less like a military stronghold.

75) Visit a shipwrecked and haunted ship.

Now, the shipwrecked part we know for sure, the haunted part is just legend. But the rumor is that the remains of the S.S. San Pasqual were never recovered due to rumors that the wreck was haunted. The ship was launched from San Diego in 1920 and was damaged in a storm in 1922. The ship was later purchased to store sugar cane until she sunk in 1933, still full of sugar cane! This is where the haunted rumors come in—no one wanted to recover the contents of the ship for fear that perhaps it was riddled with ghosts, so the sugar remained in the ship until it fermented into rum! A sailor's dream boat! They say you still smell the rum!

76) View some neo-caveman art. What's that

you say? You've never heard of neo-caveman art? You're not alone. But if you take a chance on it, you will be fascinated by the elaborate and beautiful cave paintings done by Morillo in the Vinales Valley. The colorful world history painting spans an expansive rock wall. The project took years to finish, and a lot more money than originally estimated, but since its completion, people have been enjoying the beautiful work Morillo executed. It is definitely worth the trip to see it.

77) Stand in oversized history.

Bacona Park is right outside of Santiago de Cuba, which is known as the Cradle of the Revolution—where it all happened! Bacono Park has created attractions to celebrate the victories and beauties of Cuba's past. But they didn't start at the revolution! No, they started at the very beginning and there are 200 dinosaurs roaming in the park! There are tropical scenes, bars, model cars and a museum fully dedicated to the attack on

Moncada. This odd park is a walk through history that you won't want to miss!

78) Look at this old lookout tower.

Built in 1750 to keep watch on the slaves working in the sugar cane fields, the Manaca Iznaga tower is 7 stories high, with 136 steps to the top. The view today is much better than that of its inception. Today, rather than watching slaves at work, you can see a truly remarkable view of the entire valley, plus get a good workout while walking up those steps!

79) See the highest point in Cuba.

The highest peak in Cuba got a little higher in 1953 when a bust of Jose Marti—Cuban poet and politician—was erected at its peak. The revolutionary figure dedicated his life to liberating Cuba from Spain, and his statue is a monument honoring his work for the revolution.

80) See a national monument.

Pay a visit to the Tren Blindado. This national monument is a memorial park and museum in honor and remembrance of the Cuban Revolution. If you feel like there are a lot of tributes and monuments to the revolution—you are correct. It's a huge part of Cuban history. I personally like to plan my days thematically, so I suggest planning a day or two to try and check out all of the monuments to the Revolution that you want to see.

81) Go pedal boating.

Josone Park is a picturesque park with a wide selection of bars and restaurants as well as a swimming pool, pedal boats and a beautiful bridge to boat under. It is the perfect place for a peaceful afternoon and maybe even a picnic. A light selection in a land with a lot of dark opportunities.

82) See human remains.

The Varahicacos Ecological Reserve has been a designated nature preserve since 1974. A visit here offers you the opportunity to see 2,500 year-old human remains and ancient pictographs in aboriginal caves. It's a fascinating step into the past in a fabulously beautiful outdoor setting. An odd excursion and a great day trip out of the city!

83) See where Fidel Castro was born.

In 1926, Fidel Castro Ruz was born at Finca las Manacas. Today, tours are available for those who are interested in seeing and learning more about the birthplace of the notorious leader. The city and the house itself have become heavy tourist destinations, with interested people flocking to the place where it all began.

84) To the lighthouse!

The iconic lighthouse of Castillo de lods Santos Reyes Magnos de Morro was built between the years of 1589 and 1630. It as erected as a measure of security for the entrance to the Havana harbor, protecting it from pirates and invaders. It is a fabulous example of Renaissance military architecture. The beautiful lighthouse is a very worthwhile destination.

85) Get artsy.

This multi-purpose art exhibit was founded by Afro-Cuban fusion musician X-Alfonso. The Fabrica de Arte Cubano is a venue for live music, art expos, fashion shows and other art collaborations. This place is very hip and happening at the moment. There are a lot of possibilities for great exhibitions, so keep your eyes on this place for exciting opportunities. If you are lucky there will be a special exhibition during your visit. But even if there is not, there is still plenty to see and you'll be glad you went.

86) Get a little bit everything.

At Club Majunje there is something for everyone. You can dabble in urban graffiti, a childrens theater, crooners, salsa dancing and even a drag show. This place fits the bill if you're looking for a place where everyone can find something they like. It's not your typical one size fits all place, but it's bursting with personality and opportunities so why not go ahead and give it a shot!

Chapter 8: On Film

Because for so long we had no personal access to Cuba, all we had to base our dreams on was what we saw in films. This was enough to create a wanderlust for the city within the hearts and minds of many of us. I also find that through films we learn the essence of a place—real or imagined. We get a feel for a city of culture and it either alarms us because it is so different, or it enchants us and calls to us to visit.

I think the latter here is the situation we find ourselves interested in visiting Cuba. It seems so far away but on film we have a little slice of it—a little taste. We are able to see a snippet into a world that is otherwise kept away from us. These are some of the films that offered Cuba to us during the many years we are unable to see for ourselves. I suggest watching as you plan your trip, just to entice you even more.

87) Our Man in Havana.

Filmed in 1959, this film was made right after the revolution and before the Cuban Missile Crisis. It's a rather dark comedy that is set in the years shortly preceding the revolution. Mysteries and secrets abound but the Havana nightlife is very much alive and present.

You get a feel for the time and the urgency of the revolution. If you are planning to study the history of the Cuban Revolution and see the many monuments that there are to see while you are there, I highly recommend watching this film to get yourself into the mindset of the times.

88) Buena Vista Social Club.

This is a fantastic documentary about the rich culture of Cuban music. Named after a famed Havana Social Club where a wide selection of musicians used to play, the documentary follows musicians of Cuba, many of whom have since fallen on hard times.

It's a fantastic look at the real life and culture in Havana and is sure to inspire your sense of music and wonder. There is no shortage of great music in Cuba, in fact, quite the opposite. The documentary was named after the night club, as was a band that, like the club and the documentary both, encompasses the sounds, the vibes and the heart and soul of Havana. It must be a lucky name!

89) Brothers in Exile.

An absolute must watch if you are interested in sports or the tense relationship between the Unites States and Cuba. This is a 2014 ESPN production about Cuban baseball, the illegality of Cuban Baseball players and two Cuban brothers who fled their country to play the sport they love.

There is a lot of emotion behind this subject for so many people and none more so than those who play the sport. The option of choosing between the sport and profession you love or your home country seems like a terrible and impossible one. Watch to see the struggle of these brothers who faced that very real and scary option.

90) Havana.

Aptly named, there is no doubt that this film takes place in the heart of Cuba. A mystery of disappearances, hidden clues and some political undertones, this is definitely worth a watch. It isn't the lightest or the brightest interpretation of Havana, but it is a good film and an interesting look at the city through the eyes of mystery.

91) Una Noche.

If you brushed up on your Spanish as previously recommended, you'll know that this movie is bout "One Night." This is a heavy drama that feels very real and raw. This film isn't going to give you any warm and fuzzy feelings about Cuba, but it is renowned for its plot-heavy substance as a film.

I recommend watching this one, not for the wanderlust, but for a different approach. Plus, it's fun to see the city you are visiting on film so you can look for anything familiar while you are there.

Chapter 9: Points of Interest

There is no doubt in my mind or in yours, that if you are to visit Cuba, you are going to Havana. This is completely a given. You will fall in love with Havana. I mean, with all the music, dancing, food and drinks—you might fall in love in Havana! But Havana isn't the only major city worth a visit while you are in Cuba. Here is a list of a handful of other cities that are definitely worth a visit while you are there. They each have their own flavor of culture and personality, and you might just be surprised by what you end up enjoying most while you are in Cuba. You may not have time to visit all of them, but please do try and get to some of these cities—you won't regret it!

92) Trinidad.

Trinidad is a stunningly beautiful colonial city and a UNESCO World Heritage Site. There are no cars allowed into the city center, so it's a fantastic place to go for long, uninterrupted walks on the fabulous cobblestone streets. Markets abound and there are musicians on nearly every corner. There is a beautiful tower where you can climb to the top and see remarkable views of the city, views that will take your breath away! You will not want to miss the chance to eat in restaurants that are set in old colonial homes and to experience a wonderful atmosphere and environment. Like so much of Cuba, there are endless amounts of beautiful culture to experience.

93) Cienfuegos.

Much less visited by tourists, Cienguegos is definitely not a place to overlook. Located right on the sea, this beautiful little place is a calm escape from the hustle and bustle of the major cities.

There is a natural beauty and energy that encompasses this quiet city. There is a cemetery with tombs honoring soldiers from various independence wars. You can walk around botanical garden and different shores. Not far from the city of Cienfuegos is the Bay of Pigs, the place a lot of the more modern history revolves around. As a book lover, I would bring a nonfiction book about the Bay of Pigs to the actual location and spend a day reading and looking out over the spot. But if you're less interested in that and more interested in the pure natural beauty—opportunities for diving and snorkeling abound in this area!

94) Santiago.

The second largest city in Cuba and by far the hottest, Santiago is classic Caribbean environment. The architecture is memorable and beautiful, the music is loud and lively and there is so much to see and do! Walk around, plan a day trip and soak in everything you can. Don't forget your hat and sunscreen though! You'll always enjoy the day more if you feel your best.

95) Santa Clara.

Santa Clara's claim to fame is as the first city that was freed by the revolution in 1958. Here you can see a monument to Ernesto Che Guevara, a site that has become a pilgrimage for many visiting the city who want to honor the revolutionary hero. Coincidently Santa Clara is the city where Che's wife, Aleida March was born. It is full of music and culture, and is certainly home to a whole host of history!

96) Baracoa.

Small and a little sleepy, Baracoa is worth a visit for any of you who are eating your way through Cuba. The gourmet capital of the country, Baracoa offers a host of eateries and delicious dishes. Highly tropical, it rains nearly every day and the effects of that rain are evident on the wearing buildings. But its is a quiet city that is quite delicious and offers a host of reasons to stop by for a visit and maybe even stay a little longer than expected.

97) Camaguey.

A living labyrinth! The city of Camaguey is designed in such a way that enemies of invaders would get lost and confused in attempts to find their way around. An exciting design with a fun basis in history and an explorers dream! It is on the busier side so there are lots of little shops to visit. But be careful to trace your steps, lest you get lost along your way!

Chapter 10: Get Into the Groove

By now you have certainly picked up on the fact that the music scene in Cuba is incredible... insanely so. Maybe that is why you wanted to go to Cuba in the first place. Maybe you didn't know until you read this travel guide and now you are just hoping to finish reading soon so you can go immerse yourself in Cuban music! Either way, you should try out a full music engagement into Cuban culture.

I have listed just a few of the artists and bands that you should look into during your immersion. By no means does this encompass everything that you need to listen to, but it's a starting place. I listed both classics and some modern musicians so you can get a range of the music over the last century, but by no means should your search stop here! Check out some of the best music to come out of Cuba—it will get you in the groove for a great trip.

98) Buena Vista Social Club.

You may remember seeing this name already in this book—you are correct! A documentary film was made about this musical revolution. That being said, you should get into the music for the real feel. The band is named after the famous club, as is the film. The music is iconic and life changing, and is the epitome of Cuban music. If there is only one artist you listen to from Cuba, this group should be it. They have some of the best hits to ever come out of the country. This is a group you can't pass by. They are so good that you might get stuck here and never listen to anything else.

99) Celia Cruz.

Known for her powerful voice and super smooth rhythm-centric style—this Cuban singer is a powerhouse of vocal control. Well worth a listen, she will knock you off your feet and get you moving to the music. What I love most about Celia Cruz is that her music somehow has the ability to totally put me at ease while at the same time inspiring me. I feel both calmed and pumped up all at once. She's really an amazing artist.

100) Dayme Arocena.

This modern Cuban artist abounds in charisma and charm. Her style is so smooth that is transcends any one genre. But she excels in jazz. You'll find a lot of her music is very popular right now so I wouldn't be surprised if you hear a lot of her music while you are in Cuba.

101) Carlos Victoriano Varela Cerezo.

Cerezo is a singer-songwriter of nueva trova from Havana, Cuba. In the 1980s, he joined the Nueva Trova musical movement, a political and poetic musical genre. Multi-faceted and incredibly musically inclined, Cerezo's music will move you and I can almost guarantee that you'll keep coming back for more.

Conclusion

I went, I saw, and I tried to stay forever. After you go, you certainly aren't the first person to visit Cuba and never want to leave, and you certainty won't be the last. The country calls to something in a traveler's heart. It is old and new and perfectly balanced.

It offers to you some of the best things that you could ever ask for—beautiful weather, beaches, rich history, loyalty, incredible food, spirited drinks, dancing, laughter and music, music, music. No wonder the people in Cuba always seem so happy—they have so much of so many good things!

Another truly beautiful thing about Cuba is

that you are there for the experience, you kind of have to be. You are there for the memories and not for the souvenirs. This may not be your first choice, but it doesn't really matter because the choice has already been made for you.

Because of the remaining trade and exchange laws, you can't bring many souvenirs home! For a long time you couldn't bring anything home, but there are current allowances for small amounts of product. So what you have to do is this—soak up the good moments and hold onto them to replay over and over.

After so long with so many travel restrictions, there aren't many people with Cuban vacation stories—but you'll have one! See it, enjoy it and toast to your trip, the memories will give you all you really need to cherish it. Is that a good deal, or what?

"Thanks for reading! If you like the book, please write a short review on Amazon with your thoughts. Also, if you like this book, please let others know, in order to share the awesomeness of this travel destination!" – James Hall

Bonus: the Secret for Cheap Flights

Did you know there are travelers who never pay for flights? Or when they pay, they pay very little.

Some are people who travel full time. Some are people with normal jobs. Some are moms and dads, others are single travelers.

They're the same as everyone else - with one big exception:

They don't pay for flights. They can travel anywhere they want, whenever they want.

So before you travel, make sure you know the 3 tips to get the cheapest flights possible.

* * *

There are 3 ways you can get cheap flights.

1) Use Error Fares

2) Use Throwaway Tickets

3) Get (Almost) Free Flights

* * *

1. Look for Error Fares

Error fares are cheap plane tickets that the airlines put up online by mistake. You can find these on websites like SecretFlying.com or AirfareWatchdog.com.

These flights can be as much as 50% below what you'd normally pay. That said, they only leave from certain destinations and only go to certain places.

* * *

2. Use Throwaway Tickets

Did you know it's sometimes cheaper to book a LONGER flight.. and throw away the second portion?

Example: Instead of booking New York to Texas, it might be cheaper to book a ticket from New York to Los Angeles, with a layover in Texas.

Just get off at the layover and discard the 2nd leg of the flight.

* * *

3. The Secret to book $1,000 flights for just $20 or less. (MOST IMPORANT)

This strategy is the easiest and most effective of the three. By using a few tricks to earn frequent flyer miles really quickly (without being a frequent flyer,) you can basically get free flights over and over and over.

As a small token of my appreciation for you reading this book, I have a FREE gift for you showing this **Secret to book $1,000 flights for just $20 or less.**

Check out the video showing you how on my website   at: www.JamesHallTravel.com/TravelHack

I hope that it would help you save money on your flight tickets like I did, so you can travel more and enjoy what life has to offer!

Enjoy!

About the author

James Hall is an American author with a deep interest and passion in travelling around the world. After a trip to Thailand in 2008, he has decided to quit his job and stayed in Thailand and became "semi-retired". He taught English in Thailand and in different Asia countries where he goes to.

He has been living in different parts of Thailand for 4 years, and has been travelling all over Asia and around the world.

As an avid traveler, James' goal is to give readers all the essential information for travelling based on his own experience. His passion is to give others inspirations to go explore the world

Check out my other books...

Thailand

ULTIMATE TRAVEL GUIDE
TO THE BEST OF THAILAND

JAMES HALL

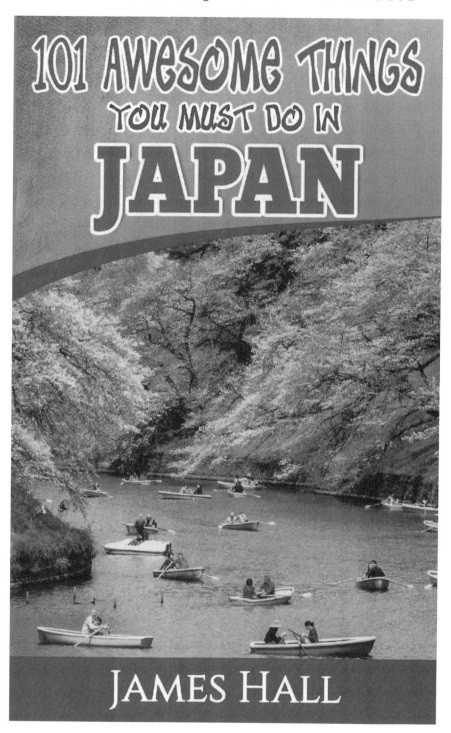

101 AWESOME THINGS YOU MUST DO IN IRELAND

JAMES HALL

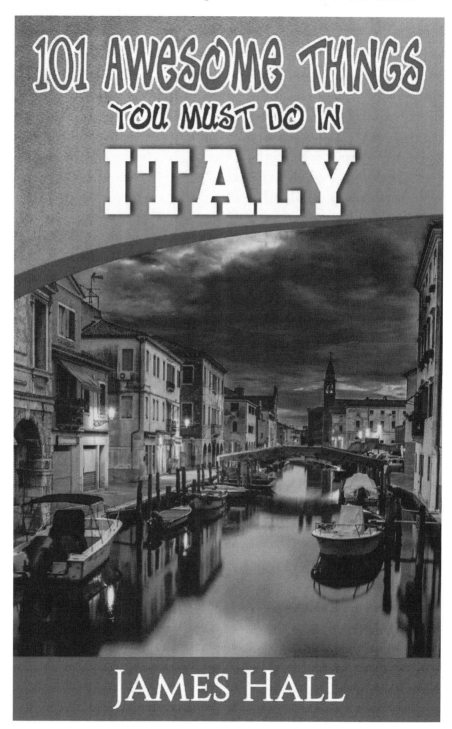

101 AWESOME THINGS
YOU MUST DO IN
COSTA RICA

JAMES HALL

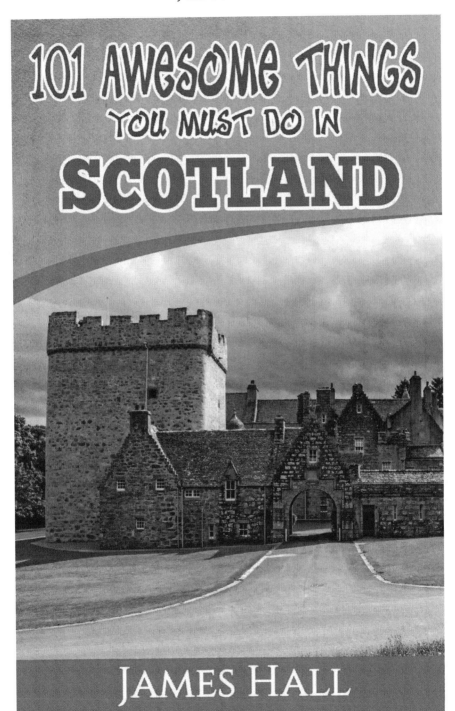

101 AWESOME THINGS YOU MUST DO IN SCOTLAND

JAMES HALL

Still interested in my other travel books?

I have many more to come. I intend to write about all the places that I traveled to.

Connect with me on my website at www.JamesHallTravel.com, or check out my Amazon Author Page for my new books: https://www.amazon.com/James-Hall/e/B01M5K2N8F.